★★★★ *THE SKILLS OF ORGANIZING* ★★★★

PUBLIC FRIENDSHIP

William L. Droel

PUBLIC FRIENDSHIP
by William L. Droel

Edited by Gregory F. Augustine Pierce
Cover and text design and typesetting by Patricia A. Lynch

Copyright © 2013 by William L. Droel

Published by ACTA Publications, 4848 N. Clark Street, Chicago, IL 60640, (800) 397-2282, www.actapublications.com, in cooperation with the National Center for the Laity, PO Box 291102, Chicago, IL 60629

All rights reserved. No part of this publication may be reproduced or transmitted in any form or by any means, electronic or mechanical, including photocopying and recording, or by any information storage and retrieval system, including the Internet, without permission from the publisher. Permission is hereby given to use short excerpts or pieces of art with proper citation in reviews and marketing copy, church bulletins and handouts, and scholarly papers.

ISBN: 978-0-87946-506-3
Printed in the United States of America by Total Printing Systems
Year 22 21 20 19 18 17 16 15 14 13
Printing 15 14 13 12 11 10 9 8 7 6 5 4 3 2 First

♻ Text printed on 30% post-consumer recycled paper

CONTENTS

★★★★

A Note from the Publisher / 5

Introduction / 9

Social Networks / 13

Middle Ring Relationships / 25

Disciplines and Virtues / 35

The Powerful 2% / 43

Sources / 47

A NOTE FROM THE PUBLISHER

★★★★

Bill Droel and I are friends. Both public friends (we work together on a variety of public issues and organizations) and private friends (he introduced me to my wife, Kathy.) So when Bill asked me to publish his essay on Public Friendship, what else was I supposed to do?

Like most things Bill writes, *Public Friendship* is not only well-written but also timely and insightful and helpful to anyone who wants to be both faithful and effective in public life.

We are becoming a nation of strangers who practice a frustrating type of democracy. We see the results everywhere from Washington to Wall Street to Main Street. We are no longer friends who disagree; we are strangers who refuse to communicate—and democracy without communication is like marriage without intimacy.

Bill Droel has spent his life in and around social justice (he wrote the book on it, called *What Is Social Justice*, which is another in this series of booklets). He has been the driving force behind the National Center for the Laity, based in Chicago, for over thirty years. He has worked in campus ministry, as a pastoral associate, and as an instructor at Moraine Valley Community College in the southwest suburbs of Chicago. He has been involved in more causes than Google has gigabytes.

So he knows firsthand the skills that are needed in public life, especially the ability to make and sustain what he calls "public friendships" in order to bring people together on social justice efforts. Let me say that the phrase *public friendship* was not known to me before I read Bill's manuscript, but it feels much better than "public relationships" or "mutual self-interest" or even "relational organizing." For public friendship is the perfect metaphor for what we are trying to accomplish by building intentional relationships with one another so that we might go into action together to make the world a better place for all.

I myself have had hundreds, perhaps thousands, of public friends over the years. These are people who I got to know through various organizations. A few of them turned into personal friends as well, but most of them remained public. That means I don't necessarily invite them to my kids' baptisms and weddings, but we do invite and challenge one another to work on issues we all care about.

For example, Oussama Jammal and Mimi Ko and Alec Harris and Maggie Perales and Rev. Al Ragland and Amy Totsch and Richard Fung and Kathleen Kearns and Arturo Gonzales and Christine Pope and a host of other Chicagoans from a variety of religious traditions (and some with no religious tradition at all) are public friends of mine and of one another. We have worked together for over a decade through an organization called United Power for Action and Justice. We truly like and trust one another, and we are certainly friendly when we get together. We care about one another's welfare and families and work lives, but we get together to do public business on health care and affordable housing and gun violence and other issues we cannot solve individually or through our own individual networks and institutions. We are public friends. Our friendship is (mostly) public.

Bill Droel explains not only why such public friendships are important in a democracy but also how to go out and make them. He even finishes with a few tips on the "virtues" necessary to sustain them. If there is anything that we need to pass on to the next generation, it is this. So thanks to my public (and private) friend for providing this resource for anyone—young, middle-aged, or old—who wants to learn the art of public friendship.

Gregory F. Augustine Pierce
President and Co-Publisher
ACTA Publications

INTRODUCTION

★★★★

My college students are surprised to hear me say that friendship is essential to social change. It is not what I would have taught as a younger teacher or activist. Looking back, however, it is clear to me that any success on race relations, labor justice, business ethics, the dignity of life, and other social change is dependent on webs of one-to-one relationships that are strong enough to be called public friendships. Further, as specific issues come and go, public friendship is a sustaining factor in social progress.

Many of the ideas in this booklet apply to all types of friendships: the intimate friendship between spouses, the sometimes casual friendship of drinking buddies or college classmates, accidental friendships with neighbors and members of religious institutions and bowling leagues, intense and sometimes volatile friendships among siblings and parents and their adult children, short-term and long-term friendships with colleagues and fellow employees at work. And obviously, some specific friends fall into more than one type of friendship. The specific focus in this booklet, however, is on public friendship: how it is developed and how it works to bring about change in our society.

Aristotle's notion of *philia* includes this public friendship (although he puts a few other friendship types in the *philia* category). *Philia* goes beyond merely liking someone or sharing a mutual interest in a sports team or a hobby. *Philia* is appreciation of another person's character and well-being. Because Aristotle insists that people are social by nature, *philia* takes into account the environment or institutions that shape the friendships that we really care about. Ultimately then, *philia* is concern for the public good, the *polis*.

In this regard Aristotle also wrote about *homonoia* or political friendship. The word *political* as he used it (and as it will be used in this booklet) is not restricted to electoral politics. Unfortunately, English phrases for *homonoia* are out of favor; words like *concord*, *civic affection*, *camaraderie*, *trust* or perhaps what Thomas Jefferson meant by the unalienable right to pursue *civic happiness*.

Aristotle assumed a vibrant commitment to public friendships in his depiction of the *polis*. Free people interested in a healthy society, he believed, understand the necessity of regular face-to-face conversations among citizens that lead to long-term relationships.

Some public figures today act as if hundreds of people are their good buddies. These public personalities are adept at working the crowd at a banquet, proficient in flattering comments, seemingly interested in other people's problems. This booklet is not about them. Public friendship is not about winning friends, making an assertive presence on the job, or influencing the populace with a charming personality. Public friendship as here discussed is not utilitarian. It is a genuine, reciprocal relationship that normally unfolds over lunch in a restaurant, in office conversations, or in a church, synagogue, mosque, temple, school, or community-center meeting room. It is similar to other types of friendship, except that it intentionally expresses itself at some point in public business and usually attempts to expand the circle of like-minded people, at least to some degree.

Unlike intimate friendships, public friendship has limits. Public friends are vulnerable to one another, but in a calculating or restricted manner. Public friends do not necessarily share private information with one another. On the other hand, public friendships are not one-way. Public friends are not "supporters" or "constituents" or people on an email list serve. Public friends are friends because each is getting something out of the relationship.

Public friendship can be practiced anywhere. But cities are the noblest creation of humankind because they are the incubators in which an unlikely mixture of people and interests can craft a culture and then a civilization. Poets, taxi drivers, students, engineers, parents, property owners, nurses, immigrants, the dispossessed and politicians all create a workable environment by trading their views or, as Ed Chambers says in another booklet in this series, "by mixing their spirits." And yes, politicians who greet their constituents at a train stop or in a diner or a union hall are part of the mix, provided they really listen to specific concerns about a school, a park, a clinic, or a factory.

In a way it is odd that we have lost public friendship. After all, we live in proximity to thousands of people. We see hundreds of them in passing every day. We now have technology that allows us to connect with hundreds more around our town, our country, and across the world. Yet, few people practice the arts of public friendship today. Why is this?

Many blame the ubiquitousness of modern media. We can connect with people by telephone and cellphone, SKYPE, email, text messaging, Twitter, Facebook, YouTube, blogs, websites, television, cable, radio, audio and video downloads, and on and on. One of my longtime friends tells me he receives 400 emails a day, looks at 200, and answers 100 of them. No wonder he doesn't have time to go out for a beer anymore. He is too busy with phony relationships to work on his real ones.

The decline of public friendship is tragic because in my opinion a life of true happiness is possible only in community. The false circumstances of modern life with autonomous individuals surrounded by mega-institutions of government and business lead to anxiety, instability, insularity, loss of enchantment, and powerlessness—no matter one's material assets.

A society rich in community based on public friendships, is still possible. It requires groups of people to first reflect upon and then act on behalf of their public relationships. This is not a second-best kind of activity; something to do only if time permits or something for a few highly extroverted people. Public friendship is an exercise in truth.

William L. Droel
Chicago, Illinois

SOCIAL NETWORKS

★★★★

It is impossible to convince a sports fan that game decisions based on instant replay are no more accurate than the fallible judgment of an umpire or referee. Nor is it possible to convince anyone that instant replay has the added disadvantage of making the game less interesting. It does no good to point out that two dimensional pictures, even from multiple angles, cannot capture three-dimensional life. Of course, making game decisions based on instant replay is rapidly expanding. It is simply too frustrating for sports leagues to support the judgment of skilled officials when fans and reporters have access to replays.

For the vast majority of people, as Plato taught long ago, appearance trumps reality. Even though it is colored dots on a screen, people assume TV is reality. People even believe in *reality TV shows*, as if it is possible *not* to be an actor when in front of a camera. Fanatical sports fans now use the phrase *I was at that game* to mean *I saw the game on TV*.

Such confidence in electronic technology extends to group interaction. It was a Saturday morning meeting for a church's Human Concerns Committee. Over several years the group had launched a one-night-per-week homeless shelter in the parish gym. Plus they had an active Prayer Shawl Ministry, a brisk quarterly sale of Fair Trade products, and a solid track record of assisting individual needy families. But the steering committee meetings had become decidedly unexciting.

After the initial prayer and introductions one Human Concerns leader, using a kindly tone, said she missed the personal interaction and conviviality that the committee once enjoyed. Several others agreed with her and the meeting proceeded with better humor than in the recent past. The main agenda item was the committee's upcoming presentation on caring for aged relatives. Despite the usual announcements in the church bulletin and a mailing to a targeted segment of parishioners, registration for the program was especially low. The very same woman who earlier lamented the loss of the personal touch within the committee now spoke: "We need lots more publicity." Turning to a retired businessman in the group, she continued: "Bob, you know all about computers. Maybe you or one of your former employees can improve our parish website and get our events out there. Young adults are constantly on Facebook. We would probably attract them if we had a top notch Facebook page."

Two or three other leaders strongly affirmed her comment, but then the meeting seemed to lose its momentum. Nothing was ever done about publicity on the Internet. The program on aging parents was indeed held three weeks later with 15 participants—a respectable number, I suppose, but not a major crowd like the committee had once envisioned. It was interesting to me, and I pointed out in the evaluation session at the next meeting that *every single one* of the people who actually showed up at the program *had prior personal contact* with a specific committee member.

Here was my point. If we had spent the time we wasted dreaming about developing an "easy" solution based on modern technology and instead gone out and made more public friendships or, better yet, recruited a few other parishioners to bring *their* already existing public friendships to the service of this worthy cause, we would have had more people at the meeting and hence been more effective helping people care for their aged relatives *which was the purpose of the Human Concerns Committee.* That committee is not supposed to merely go through the motions but to effectively connect with others who might need their help.

Many church groups, school committees, ethnic or neighborhood associations, student clubs, and professional organizations have similar meetings to that of my parish's erstwhile Human Concerns Committee. They often come to the conclusion that because their membership and/or participation is declining they need more visibility in cyberspace. It seems like a logical strategy. But it must be judged on the same basis as any other strategy: Does it work?

Social networks, like computers in general, have introduced new words to our language. For example, *to friend* is a new verb, different from the verb *to befriend*. To *un-friend* is also new. It is like the verb *to sever a friendship* or *to lose a friendship*, but not quite the same.

To borrow the language of friendship for use in

social networks is not a neutral exercise, writes Diana Schaub of Loyola College in Maryland. Transplanting the idiom of friendship uproots it from its essential "moral context" and soon "debases the meaning of friendship." Drawing upon Aristotle, Schaub says that contrary to the assumption of its users, "online networking [has actually] contributed to the decline of friendship." It creates the illusion of closeness while introducing a mechanical barrier to the discipline of deliberate connections. Social networks, properly understood, are really the latest byproduct of the "radically individualistic strands in modern thought."

There is an automobile commercial that captures the contradiction of relying on the latest technology to achieve friendship. A young adult is in her apartment, laptop in front of her. She expresses concern that her parents are lonely, while she is cyber-connected to hundreds of friends. Her tone, however, betrays that she entertains doubts about intimacy in her life. Meanwhile the commercial pans to the parents, who gleefully drive the advertised automobile to destinations filled with enjoyable friends. The commercial, of course, avoids mentioning that automobiles (and especially the Interstate Highway system) also jeopardize friendships—encouraging family members to work or to move some distance from the family hearth. The automobile culture has also all but destroyed the older friendship network known as *neighborhood*.

As a college teacher, I sometimes show a cartoon to my students to make a similar point. It shows an attractive couple (a young woman and a guy) sitting knee-to-knee on a train, each holding an electronic device. Its caption asks: "Who is each person texting?" Several of my students, without any apparent irony, quickly reply: "Each other." The cartoon illustrates a paradox of the modern age: Even when we are in close proximity we communicate in person less frequently. People prefer to send messages up to a satellite in order to reach a colleague in an adjacent office, rather than walk down the hall. And, if the cartoon reflects reality, even people knee-to-knee prefer to mediate their communication through electronic devices.

People increasingly inhabit "a whole world of machine-mediated relationships on networked devices," says Sherry Turkle of MIT in her book *Alone Together*. "As technology offers us substitutes for connecting with each other face-to-face," she continues, people either hardly realize the substitution or actually prefer it—investing in inauthentic, artificial, and disembodied relationships over real live friends, leaving us "lonely despite our connections."

First, social networks change private life. "When technology engineers intimacy, relationships can be reduced to mere connections," says Turkle. Enamored with social networking devices, "people take comfort in being in touch with a lot of people whom they also keep at bay." Soon they are "unsure if they are closer together or further apart."

Public space changes too, according to Turkle. A campus or a conference, for example, could be a place to casually meet others and exchange ideas. But now most people in those settings—almost always accompanied by their laptop and cell phone—choose "to be alone with their personal networks."

A fault in our culture is thinking mechanical devices "will solve everything; [it is a] refusal to recognize the limitations of knowledge," Turkle concludes. "Technology gives us more and more of what we think we want," but not necessarily what we really need.

Mobile computers (laptops and phone-sized devices) along with their applications (apps) and social networks are popular because they allow individuals to access lots of information, including details about business associates, family members, casual acquaintances, and—best of all—"celebrities," who are people famous for being famous. These technologies also seemingly make public events and social causes more widely known, particularly to people who might not have a personal contact with leaders in the cause. Think of the millions of "friends" that computer-savvy politicians on all sides have. Therefore, social networks and mobile phones and the like contribute to the vitality of social organizations, from church committees to large movements in Egypt and elsewhere. Is this correct?

Not necessarily. Popular sociologist Malcolm Gladwell distinguishes "weak-tie activity" from "strong-tie activism." Writing in *The New Yorker*, Gladwell analyzes recent protests in the Middle East and elsewhere. Commentators highlight how the use of Facebook, Twitter, and other communication tools in these protests allow "the powerless to collaborate, coordinate, and give voice to their concerns."

These electronic tools are "in many ways a wonderful thing," says Gladwell, but many commentators have an "outsized enthusiasm for social media.... The platforms of social media are built around weak ties [that] seldom lead to high-risk activism." Social networks are good for sharing information with acquaintances and strangers. But by their nature they lessen "the level of motivation that participation requires." Young adults sign up on Facebook and the like for campaigns that don't ask too much of them: a donation, a one-time event, a vote for a candidate, or a petition-drive signature. But don't ask them to come to a meeting. They wouldn't "know" anyone!

Gladwell's main example of strong-tie activism comes from North Carolina and its nearby states in the early 1960s, where students integrated lunch counters, bus terminals, and other facilities "without e-mail, texting, Facebook or Twitter." Their activism needed ideological fervor, but it also required "personal connection" to fellow activists. And in fact, as Gladwell details, most of the civil rights leaders had prior relationships in colleges, seminaries, and churches. Changing socially entrenched norms and practices, like those in the once-segregated South, requires risky, longer term involvement. Real social change agents are subject to discouragement, ostracism from colleagues and even family, possibly arrest, and beatings in some cases. Long-haul, risky activism, Gladwell concludes, depends on strong-tie friends supporting one another.

There is no denying that the Internet played a significant role in the 2011 movements for democracy in the Middle East. However, technology's place in the story is complex. Wael Ghonim, a prominent leader of the movement in Egypt, is an executive with Google—now on leave of absence. He is a big fan of Internet technology. He met his wife online. He made money from programs and sites he devised. Ghonim formed a close partnership with another movement leader, Abdelrahman Mansour, without ever meeting him in person. "I find virtual life in cyberspace quite appealing," Ghonim writes. "I prefer it to being visible in public life."

His initial role was to launch a Facebook group in order to "market" opposition to the government. Prior to the mass rallies, his electronic group had thousands of users. It was useful for gauging the potential strength of planned actions and in evaluating what happened. Thus to Ghonim the events in Egypt are "definitely an Internet revolution." Ghonim concludes: "If you want a free society, just give people Internet access."

It is not accurate, however, to conclude from this one account that the Arab Spring in Egypt was a creation of the Internet or that the Internet was the primary tool of the protestors. The events of early 2011 were long in the making. The 2011 protest in Egypt "was organized by a surprisingly small clique" of young professionals, says foreign affairs reporter Robin Wright. They had "limited—and largely unsuccessful—political experience," although some had been previously detained or arrested. These young adults—engineers, lawyers, computer specialists—originally met during their student days. Their initial friendships allowed them to negotiate their religious and ideological differences as they brokered coalitions based on a common goal.

Ghonim and others often used the Internet to trick the police, rather than to aid communication within the movement. Of course, events eventually took on a life of their own. But for months, the leadership frequently used the Internet to propagate disinformation.

Wright concludes that communication technology contributed about a quarter of the fuel to the events in Egypt. She notes other crucial ingredients, including a large literacy gap, a declining median age, rising expectations among young adults, and visible corruption of officials and prominent business people.

Another fallacy about Internet organizing is to conclude that individuals one-by-one walked away from their keyboards to a mass rally—carrying a cell phone to keep current with events. Actually, the movement drew heavily upon the leadership of many existing groups, including the Muslim Brotherhood, the Arab Doctors Union, Coptic churches, mosques, writers' circles, trade unions, professional associations, alumni groups, and even soccer clubs. To dispel this fallacy in another way is to state that only a fraction of the Egyptian populace has Internet access. Even Ghonim admits that "reaching working-class Egyptians [is] not going to happen through the Internet."

Movements for change might appear spontaneous, but they usually rely upon pre-existing public friendships. This was true, for example, in April 1775 when Paul Revere rode his horse to Lexington and Concord to alert the revolutionaries. Contrary to "the popular image of solitary hero-figures," the entire American Revolution is a story about small, grassroots organizations, writes David Fischer of Brandeis University. Revere was hardly a lonesome rider. During those days, about 60 members of the Sons of Liberty acted as horseback messengers. Nor did Revere and the others "spread the alarm merely by knocking on individual farmhouse doors. They awakened the institutions of New England." They enlisted churches, family networks, and clubs. Revere himself belonged to five lodges in the Boston area. The same is true of the other leaders in our revolution.

Gladwell also considers effectiveness in his distinction between weak-tie activity and strong-tie activism. Weak-tie groups with a high degree of reliance on the Internet and on social networks are not capable of sustaining long-term social action, he contends. A social change effort driven by the openness of cyberspace simply "can't think strategically." If all participants in an electronic network continually have "an equal say" on everything, such groups cannot "make difficult choices about tactics or strategy or philosophical direction." It doesn't take long for the effort to dissipate or lose its edge.

The Occupy Wall St. movement, for example, mirrored many of the values of the Internet culture—at least when the Internet avoids over-commercialization. Indeed, some things about Occupy Wall Street were positive and suggestive. It showed that ordinary people who act in public can modify public discourse. The movement's insistence on full participation meant devising hand signals and employing a veto mechanism. Occupy Wall Street was a reminder that true democracy must be inclusive and accountable to its participants. Its caution about alliances with older and perhaps calcified groups speaks to the importance of fresh ideas in attracting new people and the necessity of allowing new people to share fresh ideas.

But Occupy Wall Street ultimately faded because it was with exceptions a collection of individuals drawn together by information, not by pre-existing friendships. If Occupy Wall Street was, in fact, a first step occasion for forming public friendships, the movement may well reappear in more focused form.

I am not trying to make a complete, frontal assault on computers. I use the Internet every day. My critique applies equally to posters displayed around campus. It applies to leaflets distributed in the neighborhood. It applies to announcements in the church bulletin and in local newspapers. It applies to mailings and phone banks to "targeted" lists. Media has a place in organizing, but it easily becomes a useless and distracting shortcut. There is no substitute for building time-consuming, one-to-one, relational public friendships.

Many reflective young adults already grasp this truth. After all, the real goal of social change efforts is not the issue of the day but the creation of a relational culture that sustains positive values. The means and the goal of social change are really the same; the process is the purpose. Worthwhile social change is not about substituting one surface appearance for more artificiality. Social change is about a new reality; a culture of genuine moral encounters.

MIDDLE-RING RELATIONSHIPS

★★★★

For many months, the United States Army ran a commercial under the theme "An Army of One." Each version of the ad shows an isolated serviceman or woman flying a jet, tracking on radar, aiming a high-powered gun and more. The intended message is that each enlistee will receive individually tailored training and assignments in the Army, which he or she can later parley into a career.

"When I first saw this *Army of One* slogan on TV, I could not believe my eyes or ears," writes Michael Gecan, the co-director of the Metro IAF organizing network. "I wasn't even sure I understood it at first. But I think it means that each soldier is so well equipped, so well trained, and so well supported that he can and should think of himself as able to have a direct and deadly relationship with the enemy—no matter how numerous, how passionate, and how dangerous. Of course, *An Army of One* seems to contradict what lies at the very heart of why soldiers fight and die: their relationship to their country, to their platoon, to the people they entered with, trained with, drank with, and are now fighting together with."

Gecan's father was a wounded World War II veteran. "*An Army of One* would have made little sense to my father or his platoon," he reflects. "But it makes perfect sense in 21st-century America because it reinforces the theme of personal autonomy and potency, because it reduces the dependence on other institutions and structures, and because it carries the rhythms of religious and economic individualism to their cultural (not logical) conclusion."

Sociologist Robert Putnam of Harvard University tracks participation in these "middle-ring" *little platoons* of life: VFW groups, churches, clubs, community organizations and other groups where public friendship is found and nurtured. He finds a steady decline in membership rates and levels of participation in professional associations, labor unions, parent-teacher associations, civic clubs, and virtually all other voluntary organizations. This trend amounts to a loss of "social capital" with serious repercussions for society, Putnam concludes.

Putnam's argument caught the popular imagination when he reported in his book, *Bowling Alone*, that "more Americans are bowling today than ever before, but bowling in organized leagues has plummeted." The image of the *lonely bowler* has since become emblematic of the decline in public friendship.

Putnam measured all possible reasons why people are less involved in voluntary associations and civic life: more women are in the workforce, all workers are spending more hours on the job, more time spent commuting, and many more. None of his hypotheses proved conclusive. It turns out for example that women who work outside the home are more involved in voluntary groups than full-time homemakers. Putnam, after crunching plenty of numbers, concludes that the single most significant variable is the amount of time spent watching TV. People are not disengaged because of increased pressures on the job or because of responsibilities to elderly relatives or several other more obvious explanations. It is simply because people prefer watching TV (including reality shows) to participating in the realities of ethnic clubs or PTAs or church committees. "Each additional hour of TV viewing per day," Putnam estimates, "means roughly a ten per cent reduction in most forms of civic activism." At the moment a person in the United States, on average, spends four hours and 39 minutes per day watching TV. This includes TV programs on cathode tube sets, flat screens, and computer monitors, tablets, and cell phones. Hours spent on the Internet, including on social networks, also likely erode civic participation.

A few people are concerned about the content of TV programs or Internet clips. The consequences of TV, however, are only secondarily related to the type of program being broadcast or watched. The real factor is simply time. The more hours spent in front of the screen, the less time and energy for reading, praying, interacting, exercising, joining civic groups, or even sleeping. Thus, to generalize, electronic screens (big and small) are enemies of public friendship. Conversely, the first and primary step toward better interpersonal engagement is to reduce the number of hours used watching them.

For Putnam, the retreat from middle-ring voluntary groups is a symptom of the unrelenting individuation that is part of modernity. Over the past 60-some years, this individualism has nearly replaced all "old world" types of community buffer groups. In those days of long ago it was easier to participate in these middle-ring relationships. It required walking down the block to the precinct office, the parish hall, the lodge, the school meeting room, or any comparable outpost of public friendship. In the past, foreign observers of United States culture like Alexis de Tocqueville and Jacques Maritain marveled at our plurality of voluntary associations. None would do so today. They would write about the Internet.

It is true that self-help and support groups of all kinds dot our cultural landscape. They might partially be replacing the VFW groups, clubs, and neighborhood groups of days gone by. Self-help groups, however, are not social change groups, which is the topic of this booklet. In fact, self-help groups betray their beautiful benefit whenever they reach too far beyond the needs of their individual members.

It is also true that many large, single-interest voluntary organizations are thriving, including AARP, Sierra Club, or the National Rifle Association. These groups do engage in social change, but are not based upon public friendship. Their members primarily participate by donating money and lobbying by mail, telephone, or Internet at the behest of their paid leaders.

And in fairness to my caution about the Internet, it is true that at least one study says that Internet users are more likely than others to be involved in our country's organizational life. The evidence, please note, does not say that use of the Internet causes public involvement. Nor does it mean that the involvement by Internet users is in face-to-face groups. Any positive relation between the Internet and voluntary associations refers to a boost in national single-interest lobby groups.

I am not suggesting that today's activists set out to revive men's clubs in churches or reinvigorate the fraternal groups that lunch in the local restaurant. Some people will continue to socialize through such groups and should be allowed to do so undisturbed. Nor does this booklet claim that all voluntary groups of the past fostered social change. Indeed, some unions in years past put barriers between blacks and careers in the trades. Parish organizations here and ethnic clubs there led anti-integration campaigns. Attention to parochial institutions must recognize that they sometimes produce narrow-minded citizens. However, it more often happened that people raised in a secure parochial environment became sensitive to the rights and needs of others and supported progressive social policies. The genius of our country's motto, *E Pluribus Unum*, is that people who feel supported in their familiar environment develop into more effective and open-minded citizens as they enter diverse workplace and civic settings.

Totally public organizations or businesses, what are called "outer-ring" organizations, are based on achievement, competencies, and defined roles. They are not necessarily unfriendly places: Customers are treated respectfully, coworkers sometimes become close friends.

It is simply that these organizations have replaceable parts, measured against a purely bottom-line-oriented measurable goal.

Solitary individuals are at the opposite end of these large corporate organizations. They make their own choices. A family is usually part of an individual's inner-ring, yet simultaneously it is a half-step toward the middle-ring. A family demands some loss of autonomy and some regard for others. At the same time a family usually bestows total acceptance and understanding—although it is possible to get kicked out of one's family.

It is the middle-ring groups that stand fully halfway between mega-forces of society and the family. They simultaneously allow people to experience belonging and to make a difference in the wider community. Some groups emphasize belonging (what Putnam calls *bonding social capital*); they have plenty of social events. Other groups emphasize making a difference (what Putnam terms *bridging social capital*); they have lots of meetings. Some bonding groups can become too casual and risk squandering people's time and creativity. To their detriment some bridging groups can become too procedural and risk losing their relevancy. All middle-ring groups need to have an appropriate mix of belonging and making a difference, less they deteriorate into cliques.

At their best, middle-ring groups are schools of life that contribute to the moral formation of people who recognize that true self-regard actually pushes them into regard for others. This is not an easy accomplishment in our culture, overripe with materialism and individualism. The only way, however, to significantly advance the common good and societal improvement in such a climate is to build an alternative culture of public friendship.

Saddleback Church in Lake Forest, California is perhaps not an obvious example to offer to today's activists. First of all, with its 20,000 members Saddleback is larger than nearly any other middle-ring group I have discussed. Secondly, Saddleback represents an expression of Christianity that is heavy on individualism and thus in a way it reinforces the very culture many activists are trying to change.

Instead of illustrating the nature of middle-ring commitments, Saddleback has a low, noncommittal entry requirement. Weekend worshippers can remain anonymous. The service, based on market research, is tailored to the entertainment preferences of the "customers." Saddleback worship is not overly ritualistic or liturgical. People can leave without making any contribution. Its casually dressed, long-time pastor, Rick Warren, even admits that he is not into theology and so the operation sometimes appears superficial.

But look closer. To focus on Sunday is to mistake appearance for reality. Warren is an expert in sociology and his passion is for relational organizing. Saddleback, he explains, could be like any other church that starts with a small community, experiences some growth, then becomes less personal, and after that fewer people do more things around the church, until finally it goes into decline. Warren and his leaders inject a counter-dynamic into the weekend comings-and-goings of

Saddleback. They have fostered small group weekday meetings. Currently there are over 1,000 weekday Saddleback-sponsored groups—meeting either somewhere on the church's 74-acre campus or in someone's home. Through substantial participation in these small groups, the average Saddleback member, Warren explains, "knows 67 people in the congregation."

Some groups at Saddleback are mainly for faith sharing, some for self-help, and many are for outreach. The Saddleback groups, details Putnam, are heavier on *belonging* than on *making a difference*. They serve as examples for what the sociologist terms *bonding social capital*. However, as social trust has accrued in and around Saddleback, the small groups have reached outward—credibly addressing hunger in California, health care overseas, child labor, and several other issues. To that degree they are examples, says Putnam, of bridging social capital.

Putnam uses the Chicago-based Industrial Areas Foundation (IAF) to exemplify groups that are heavier on *bridging social capital*, while not neglecting *bonding social capital*. In the early 1990s, the IAF guided a process to improve grammar schools and high schools in the Rio Grande River Valley. The familiar strategy in community organizing is to "first develop a public agenda and then try to attract people." In such a strategy, parents might be cajoled or badgered to attend presentations at the school. The IAF's contrasting strategy, as Putnam details, "did not ask parents to come to the school." Instead, dedicated teachers divided up a list of parents and "made visits to students' homes, asking parents about their hopes and worries regarding the school and their children."

This slow process, says Putnam, is "called relational organizing." The families began to put their private pain into a shared context and gradually developed a vision for collective action. Abstract issues, Putnam concludes, "do not connect people." Change comes when small groups craft a story. The result was more parent participation in the education process, improved test scores, and better teacher morale. Eventually the approach spread to other schools and to an effective job training program based on the same principle of relational organizing.

In an earlier booklet in this series, Ernesto Cortes, Jr., of IAF acknowledges that the intermediate institutions that once "taught the habits and practices for a vibrant democratic culture" have withered. Into the vacuum, "the dominant market culture" has injected "alienating and homogenizing" forces that "isolate us from one another and our institutions, destroying our relationality." With the goal of rebuilding mediating institutions, the IAF wants "to assist people in slowing down, navigating and adjusting to change." In addition to its efforts in the Rio Grande Valley, Cortes draws attention to the relational organizing in Houston, New Orleans, Los Angeles and elsewhere.

DISCIPLINES AND VIRTUES

★★★★

Today's busy activists, it would seem, need guideposts along a road that winds around the twists and bends of proper interest for oneself in the context of regard for others. Those markers are the result of discipline. Such habitual behavior establishes and reinforces a person's virtue or character, allowing him or her to stay alert to signs of the times. A virtuous person, in turn, casts a spell over an area, making it easier for others to virtuously make their way.

I will mention three of the virtues that are linked to public friendship. Others could be added by the reader. These virtues of friendship are not really optional. They are not things to be done if an activist has some extra time. They are requirements for the long haul. In a serious sense, they are exercises in truth.

1. Effective Activism; the Virtue of Quietude

It may feel odd to begin a list of virtues for activists with the need for a daily and weekly routine of quiet reflection. Yet without this virtue an activist is soon caught up in activity for activity sake and in time becomes burnt out.

Too many activists, in my opinion, suffer from *partial attention disorder*, a plague affecting all of society. We flit from one thing to the next, including relationships, without pondering the meaning of it all. We catch fragments, we hear snippets, and we speak in push-button clichés. We live episodically, going from event to event without constructing the story of our own life and our lives together. We are hyper-connected, but less in touch. We are hyper-busy, but less effective.

It is not so easy to find a time and place to concentrate. Some hotels and resorts now advertise quiet rooms in which there is no TV, no DSL, and a saturated signal to block any wireless access. I was amused to learn that a company now markets Freedom software (www.macfreedom.com) which disables all Internet connection for up to eight hours on a designated computer. (Hasn't anyone heard of the "off" button?) Of course, these attempts at solitude are competing for attention with technology like Pocket Touch, which allows its users, perhaps over dinner, to text without actually touching their cell phone.

Like anything else that is worthwhile, reflection only happens if it is done on schedule in a sustained way. Maybe a half hour every morning before other members of the household awaken. No cell phone, no computer, no newspaper, no radio or TV. Coffee, of course. A pad of paper and a pencil perhaps. Plus a half hour every evening, again with a pad of paper or a journal on which to jot significant reflections from the day. My friend, publisher and community organizer Greg Pierce, says an hour to an hour and a half once a week is enough.

He calls it a "meeting with yourself" and insists that it be written in your weekly schedule and immediately rescheduled when it has to be cancelled.

Some people use a support group to aid their reflection. This is different from the regular lunch crowd that complains about the boss for a half hour. Support group members are public friends who gather to assist each member's reflection on his or her work or public activity. It is a circle that helps people be accountable. A support group must be disciplined, meeting perhaps monthly or no less than six times per year.

A mentoring relationship is another possible reflection tool. Again, it is different from a supervisor's critique of one's productivity. It is a way to hold one's self accountable for the quality of public life. Unfortunately, for the same reasons that public friendship in general is a scarce commodity, it is difficult to find competent mentors in the arts of solidarity. Pierce runs an informal group called Mentorship Chicago that seeks to match young mentees with willing middle-age mentors. He demands that the mentee write a weekly report to the mentor (during the mentee's weekly meeting with himself or herself) and that the two then meet for an hour each month to review the reflections.

The temptation in all areas of life is to find the perfect vacation spot, perfect job, perfect furniture, restaurant, novel, house of worship, golf club. So too with reflection. What is the perfect time of day or the ten secrets or the best guide? The only thing that matters, however, is picking something and doing it habitually—even though epiphanies are infrequent and fragmentary.

Without the discipline of quietude, people simply react to others around them and to random events. With reflection, no matter what kind it might be, people begin to intentionally change themselves so they can more effectively change the world.

2. Long Haul Activism; the Virtue of Compromise

Nearly everyone experiences some tension between idealism and realism. Social change agents tend to tip toward the ideal and thus must frequently deal with disappointments in real time. The key is not to resolve this tension, but to develop virtues that make the tension healthy. In that regard, compromise is an essential virtue for those interested in practical idealism.

Compromise enters the picture the moment one person meets another, because neither party will fully embody the ideals each imagines in the other. In the dynamics of public friendship, someone can one morning totally oppose the position of the other person only to call that afternoon and expect help on another topic. In other words, public friends do not take everything totally personally. That rule, by the way, is not restricted to public life. Many successful parents have learned not to take everything their children say totally personally.

Just as with the virtue of quietude, the enemy of compromise is perfection—seeking the perfect ally, the perfect issue, the perfect outcome. Public life has to be of a "high" standard of perfection, many activists at first think. Foundational moral principles seem to be at stake when someone chooses to take on a public cause.

And so, compromise is not usually thought of as a

virtue and is not often practiced as a discipline. In fact, many activists think of compromise as a vice, a sell out or an undesirable resolution to a situation. Yet it is a tragic activist who only knows how to relate to people who are with him or her in lockstep. Or the activist who can only rally the crowd but is incapable of defusing matters at the right moment to gain a partial advance for the cause. These highly principled activists are strong on protest but weak on politics, prone to moralizing but unschooled in the art of moral compromise. In real life, however, there can be no hope without calculated compromise.

Sir Bernard Crick (1929-2008) of the London School of Economics was concerned that overly-principled ideologies were destroying normal politics. He thought that idealistic activists who expected too much were unwittingly giving over the arena to those with less regard for values.

Crick set out to reclaim politics as "a distinct form of human activity in which conflicts among interests are adjudicated through discussion, persuasion and debate."

This is in contrast with tyranny and terrorism—each of which righteously moralizes. Politics, Crick insists, is a modest activity. It is "a messy, mundane, inconclusive, tangled business far removed from the passion for certainty." It is simply and profoundly a belief "that the solution to the problem of order [is] conciliation rather than violence and coercion."

Societies of diverse groups and interests are held together "because they practice politics—not because they agree about *fundamentals*," says Crick. Thus the cure for corruption, unresponsive institutions, or disrespect for one's rights is more politics, not more assertions of moral superiority.

The virtue of compromise (which, by the way, immoral people are incapable of practicing) is the way to foster a politics that results in change—a little today, a little more tomorrow.

Compromise is not something to do for its own sake or on the spur of the moment. Certainly, some compromises are never worthwhile, either because what is won is not worth what was given up or because the other side doesn't live up to its side of the bargain. But those who give sustained attention to the inner nature of compromise get better at it. Too much or too little, too soon or too late—all are ineffective compromises. Sometimes the pressure has to increase, even among friends or allies. Sometimes the pressure has to be turned off.

3. Personal Encounters; the Virtue of Amicability

The essential virtue of public friendship is an appetite for and a habit of deliberately engaging in face-to-face communication, one person to another, exploring interpersonal meanings that lurk below surface appearances. This process of genuine conversation has to be cultivated, sustained, multiplied, and replenished among many people over many days and years. The process of one-to-one interaction is an application of the soft arts of listening and reflecting. It grows as either party to the initial public friendship introduces the other to someone else. Therein resides the potential for synergy, as in the expression "paying it forward."

This booklet, let us be clear, is not promoting a technique. Our society has enough Sophists who promote techniques for winning friends and selling products. Public friendship is not an interview—one person answering another's stock questions. There is no script. Instead, two people (and then three and four) with some calculation make themselves vulnerable to one another. It is not mutual therapy. Instead, it is an exploration of mutual interests or passions; one attempt to understand why people tick. Its aim is public friendship, not intimacy. If the relationship clicks, it is intended to lead to public action, no matter how modest.

The virtue of public encounter is different from most daily interactions which are task-oriented: How will this connection help with my job, with my home repairs, my menu choice, my test scores, my other needs? "Much of what passes for relationship in the public arena is merely politeness and getting along," says Ed Chambers in an earlier booklet in this series.

The first few times activists try to conduct a one-to-one meeting they will, upon reflection, realize that it probably was a pleasant exchange of information. That's a positive start, but a genuine public friendship has to be an exchange of personal stories. It is a process-oriented interaction that makes space for "why" questions. Sincere one-to-one relationships, Chambers concludes, are "the only hope for the long-term survival and triumph of democracy."

CONCLUSION: THE POWERFUL 2%

★★★★

To be an activist is always to be a minority. That is not a discouraging fact. Keep in mind that a powerful 2% is the fulcrum that changes the world.

Maybe you first get involved because you experience an injustice. You realize, for example, that some children are being abused. Or a family member battles cancer and you fear it was caused by air pollution. Or someone's inherent dignity is disrespected because of that person's lifestyle or sexual orientation. Or a coworker is fired arbitrarily.

Let's start with any one of these experiences. Your impulse to do something is very positive, because you are sympathizing with someone other than yourself. The activist who desires to turn this initial empathy into effective, sustained action then has to find the root of this impulse in his or her own experience. The Lord, speaking in Exodus 22 (and repeating this crucial insight twice more in the Pentateuch), explains that the motivation for compassion resides in personal experience of grief, oppression, or—in the case of the Exodus audience—slavery.

Activists ask themselves and their public friends: What unresolved grief, what personal injustice, or what inner passion is my compassionate impulse touching? This is not a matter of psychotherapy. Nor is it something that has to be accomplished all at once. It is crucial, however, to be in touch with one's soul. As we improve our understanding of the impulse to act, we become more effective and we become more alert to social justice as a lifelong vocation.

Second, notice those around you. Did you begin to frame an experience into an action plan because of a conversation? Are you more confident about your impulse because someone else shares it? Can you recruit a neighbor or a family member or a schoolmate to the cause? In other words, the initial experience of need or injustice evolves into effective action as people aggregate—realizing that each person brings somewhat different interests and different degrees of passion about the particular issue.

Jane Addams (1860-1935) was idealistic as a young adult. She formulated a plan for launching a settlement house. But her renowned Hull House almost didn't materialize. Isolated from other dreamers, Addams felt paralyzed; she couldn't take the first step. Then she shared her plan with a friend, Ellen Gates Starr (1859-1940). Although Starr is nearly lost to history, she stayed with Addams and their public friendship was the key to what became a standard approach to assisting immigrant families.

Third, begin to understand that the deeper cause of the problem is not entirely material. Global warming, racism, poverty, and the like have economic dimensions. But beyond the surface appearance of economics and politics, all these issues are symptoms of a paucity of genuine connections, of the lack of solidarity, of a surplus of individualism. For example, education does not improve in a school simply because a municipality allocates more money to that school. Poverty does not go away simply because money is redistributed to select populations. A workplace does not automatically become humane because workers win a wage increase.

Improvements come because people connect with one another—genuinely, not superficially. We can mistake appearance for true reality by concluding that the best strategy on an issue is to line up all the bad guys on one side of a park and all the good guys on the other, march to the middle of the park, yell at the other side for a while, and then shake hands and proclaim that the problem is solved. In this scenario, one social problem endlessly replaces the previous one.

Only when public friends move beyond opinions to shared stories to targeted action can there be an accurate analysis of how to tackle an issue seriously. The solution to real victories is always retail organizing.

We live in a culture of irony, whose best friend is cynicism. It is a culture where those who take communication seriously are *squares* or *losers*. Thus, to make a difference in the world it is necessary, writes Christy Wampole of Harvard University, to opt out of the competition to see who cares the least. The alternative is a disciplined cultivation of public arts: "the art of conversation, the art of looking at people, the art of being seen, the art of being present." The alternative is, if you will, public resistance to irony. That means, Wampole says, virtues like "subtlety, finesse, grace, attention…sincerity, humility, and self-effacement." She correctly concludes that "people who move things in the political landscape, regardless of the sides they choose, are never ironists."

Politics should not be simply equated with electioneering and with government officials. Politics in a wider sense is the art of getting along and making improvements in public life. In that sense, says Garrison Keillor of *A Prairie Home Companion*, "politics is the best way there is to meet people and get to know who they are. Deep down, politics is about civility and about friendship, about the bonds between people."

SOURCES

★★★★

Aristotle. *Nicomachean Ethics*. Penguin Group, 2004

Aristotle. *Politics*. Barnes and Noble Library, 2005

Chambers, Edward. *The Power of Relational Action*. ACTA Publications, 2009

Cortes Jr., Ernesto. *Building Our Institutions*. ACTA Publications, 2010

Crick, Bernard. *In Defense of Politics*. University of Chicago Press, 1962

Fischer, David. *Paul Revere's Ride*. Oxford University Press, 1994

Gecan, Michael. "Taking Religion Seriously" in *Boston Review*, 9/08

Ghonim, Wael. *Revolution 2.0*. Houghton Mifflin, 2012

Gladwell, Malcolm. "Small Change" in *The New Yorker*, 10/4/10

Morozov, Evgeny. *The Net Delusion: the Dark Side of Internet Freedom*. Public Affairs, 2011

Putnam, Robert. *Bowling Alone: the Collapse and Revival of American Community*. Simon & Schuster, 2000

Putnam, Robert & Lewis Feldstein. *Better Together: Restoring American Community*. Simon & Schuster, 2003

Schaub, Diana. "Unfriending Friendship" in *Claremont Review of Books*, Spring 2011

Turkle, Sherry. *Alone Together: Why We Expect More from Technology and Less from Each Other*. Basic Books, 2011

Wampole, Christy. "How To Live Without Irony" in *New York Times*, 11/18/12

Wright, Robin. *Rock the Casbah: Rebellion across the Islamic World*. Simon & Schuster, 2011

OTHER RESOURCES ON ORGANIZING

ACTION CREATES PUBLIC LIFE
by Edward T. Chambers
Ed Chambers, the successor to Saul Alinsky and an organizer for over 55 years, mulls about the need for human beings to develop their "Public life." He argues that it is by taking action that we define who we are as adults and help create the world-as-it-could-be. Written for those who want to participate in shaping society rather than sit around and complain about things. 35-page paperback, $5.95

THE POWER OF RELATIONAL ACTION
by Edward T. Chambers
Ed Chambers talks about the building of relationships in public life that allow us to share our values, passions and interests with one another—what he calls "mixing human spirits." He describes the art of the relational meeting or "one-to-one," which he helped developed and which is now being used by clergy, leaders and organizers around the United States and in several other countries to build their congregations and community institutions and to take joint action for the common good. 33-page paperback, $5.95

THE BODY TRUMPS THE BRAIN
by Edward T. Chambers
The former executive director of the Industrial Areas Foundation (IAF) looks at how humans learn with all their senses—including instinct and intuition—and how our educations system tries to downplay what he calls "social knowledge" in favor of academic exercises. 48-page paperback, $5.95

AVAILABLE FROM BOOKSELLERS OR CALL 800-397-2282
WWW.ACTAPUBLICATIONS.COM

OTHER RESOURCES ON ORGANIZING

REFLECTING WITH SCRIPTURE ON COMMUNITY ORGANIZING
by Rev. Jeff Krehbiel
The pastor of the Church of the Pilgrims in Washington, D.C., and co-chair of the Washington Interfaith Network offers reflections on four passages from Scripture and how they relate to the experience of community organizing. He also offers a Group Study Guide for congregational use.
60-page paperback, $5.95

EFFECTIVE ORGANIZING FOR CONGREGATIONAL RENEWAL
by Michael Gecan
The author of *Going Public* and co-executive director of the Industrial Areas Foundation describes how the tools of organizing can and are transforming Protestant, Catholic, Jewish and Muslim congregations. Included are five case studies of congregations that have used this process to grow.
54-page paperback, $5.95

REBUILDING OUR INSTITUTIONS
by Ernesto Cortes, Jr.
Ernie Cortes, the co-executive director of the Industrial Areas Foundation, argues that community organizing cultivates the practices needed for democracy to thrive, including one-on-one relational meetings, house meetings, and systematic reflection on them afterwards. This book contains several examples from organizations in California, Louisiana, and Texas that helped local congregations and other mediating institutions identify, confront, and change things that were destroying their families and communities.
30-page paperback, $5.95

AVAILABLE FROM BOOKSELLERS OR CALL 800-397-2282
WWW.ACTAPUBLICATIONS.COM

OTHER RESOURCES ON ORGANIZING

STOKING THE FIRE OF DEMOCRACY
Our Generation's Introduction to Grassroots Organizing
by Stephen Noble Smith
Stephen Smith is a voice from and for the next generation of fighters for social justice. Here he explains how "could-be radicals" can recruit and support new leaders, turn isolated anger into targeted action, and—more than anything—muster the courage to make mistakes and learn from them.
123-page hardcover, $19.95

AFTER AMERICA'S MIDLIFE CRISIS
by Michael Gecan
Michael Gecan paints a vivid picture of civic, political, and religious institutions in decline, from suburban budget crises to failing public schools, what he describes as "a national midlife crisis." He shows how local organizational efforts can create vibrant institutions that truly serve their constituents and preserve and advance their communities.
128-page hardcover, $14.95

ROOTS FOR RADICALS
Organizing for Power, Action and Justice
by Edward T. Chambers
Ed Chambers' description of the "universals" of organizing. Demonstrates how to make connections across differences of nationality, culture and class. Offers practical ideas and examples for the development of citizen and congregational power. 152-pages hardcover, $12.95

AVAILABLE FROM BOOKSELLERS OR CALL 800-397-2282
WWW.ACTAPUBLICATIONS.COM

OTHER RESOURCES ON ORGANIZING

GOING PUBLIC
An Organizer's Guide to Citizen Action
by Michael Gecan
Mike Gecan, the co-executive director of the Industrial Areas Foundation and Metro IAF, tells stories and teaches lessons from his lifetime in community organizing. He explores the difference between "public" and "private," and the critical importance of building relationships as the basis for all successful, long-term organizing. Studs Terkel said, "*Going Public* is one of the most hopeful books I've read in years." 192-page paperback, $12.95

WHAT IS SOCIAL JUSTICE?
by William L. Droel
A primer by Bill Droel of the National Center for the Laity on the difference between social justice and charity, commutative justice, and distributive justice. Explains that social justice is a virtue that is practiced mostly by "insiders" of institutions, sometimes with a little help from "outsiders," and must result in the act of organizing if it is to come to fruition. 42-page paperback, $5.95

ACTIVISM THAT MAKES SENSE
Congregations and Community Organization
by Gregory F. Augustine Pierce
The classic book by Greg Pierce on why community organizing "makes sense" for parishes and congregations. Covers key issues such as self-interest, power, controversy, organization, and leadership development. 148-page paperback, $9.95

AVAILABLE FROM BOOKSELLERS OR CALL 800-397-2282
WWW.ACTAPUBLICATIONS.COM